CHOOSING A CAREER
Made Easy

CHOOSING A CAREER

Made Easy

Patty Marler ■ Jan Bailey Mattia

Printed on recyclable paper

VGM Career Horizons
NTC/Contemporary Publishing Company
Lincolnwood, Illinois USA

Library of Congress Cataloging-in-Publication Data

Mattia, Jan Bailey.
     Choosing a career made easy / Jan Bailey Mattia, Patty Marler.
       p.   cm.
     ISBN 0–8442–4343–4 (alk. paper)
     1. Vocational guidance.   I. Marler, Patty   II. Title.
HF5381.M3926   1997
331.7' 02—dc21   96–40422
                                                  CIP

Published by VGM Career Horizons, a division of NTC Publishing Group
4255 West Touhy Avenue
Lincolnwood (Chicago), Illinois 60646–1975, U.S.A.
© 1997 by NTC Publishing Group. All rights reserved.
No part of this book may be reproduced, stored in a retrieval
system, or transmitted in any form or by any means,
electronic, mechanical, photocopying, recording or otherwise,
without the prior permission of NTC Publishing Group.
Manufactured in the United States of America.
7 8 9 0 VL 9 8 7 6 5 4 3 2 1

Contents

Introduction

So, it has come to the time in your life when you have to choose a career. You may be 18 and starting to plot your career or you may be 52 and recently laid off. Either way, you are in for some change, some challenge, some soul-searching, and some work!

The times they are a changin' indeed, but with a positive attitude and an openness toward that change you will succeed. Although *Choosing a Career Made Easy* can't tell you "what to be when you grow up," it can make the journey to discovering your direction a lot less intimidating… and a lot more rewarding.

 "The life given us by nature is short, but the memory of a well-spent life is eternal."

—Marcus Tullius Cicero

Special Features

Special features throughout the book will help you pick out key points and discover new things about yourself and others.

 Notes clarify text with concise explanations.

 Helpful Hints make you stand out in the crowd applying for college.

 How'd They Get There? tells the stories of several very successful individuals, how they got where they are, and the things they plan to do next. Real people, real success stories. You're next!!

 Perspective Checks encourage you to look at your attitudes and feelings towards a variety of issues and challenge you to see other points of view.

 Interest Investigators provide suggestions on how to broaden your knowledge of careers and yourself.

 Special Thoughts provide inspiration and motivation.

Challenge yourself to make the most of you… and you will!

Chapter 1

The Evolution of "Career"

"They must often change who would be constant in happiness or wisdom."

—Confucius

It is the '90s and whether you're choosing a career for the first time or not, "career" isn't what it used to be. It is likely you will change your career at least five times during your work lifetime. How did this happen?

Historically speaking (and to a degree even today), your career choice was dictated by the amount of money your family had. If you came from a family with some disposable income and were able to finish high school and perhaps even go on to college or further education, you were lucky enough to become a professional, perhaps a doctor, lawyer, or accountant. However, if the people in your family were farmers or fishermen or tradespeople, or if you came from a large family, it was likely there was simply not enough money for you to attend college. Although a university education was certainly not as essential 70 years ago as it is today, it still did improve your career options.

Although education is considerably more accessible today, be sure you are continuing your education for the right reasons and at the appropriate time in your life.

Ultimately, "career" as we know changes with the times. It's interesting to take a short look back in history to see if it is really changing or has changed as drastically as we think.

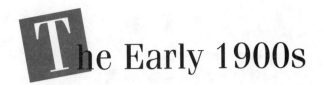# The Early 1900s

At the turn of the century and certainly into and through the 1930s, people took what jobs they could to provide for their families and were happy working when and where they could. Particularly in rural communities, a person finished school (or often didn't), got married, had a family, and proceeded to provide for that family by whatever means possible. Frequently that meant doing seasonal work, traveling to find work, or taking work of some kind into the home.

 Then, as now, *diversity* was the key. People often found themselves changing their jobs and skills as often as necessary to stay employed.

Indeed, many individuals didn't complete a formal education. There may have been work to be done on the farm, in the coal mines, or in factories and school simply wasn't as important. Job choices were limited and often hard to come by. Individuals may have stayed on the farm and inherited the land, perhaps worked in the family business, or learned a trade from a relative, close friend, or neighbor.

Very often the attitude was that if there was work to be had and money to be made, you worked whether you had completed your education or not. Regardless of job choice, work was probably seldom considered a career. It was simply the way a person made a living, and that living was something that changed and evolved out of necessity.

 Remember, there are exceptions to every generalization. Even when times were difficult, there were people who were able to stay in one career and do well.

As a great perspective check, make time to chat with your grandparents or your parents, and discover how different things were for them. Our grandparents have seen changes so huge they are hard to imagine: from education and health care to amazing advances in science and technology. With such dramatic social and technological changes in the past one hundred years, there is little question as to why people's attitudes toward work and career have had to change.

"If opportunity doesn't knock,
build a door."

—Milton Berle

The Baby Boomers

The next generation, the "baby boomers," was fortunate to be born in a postwar society that was rebuilding itself and growing in virtually every area. There were more babies born in the period between 1946 and 1964—the "boom years"—than in any earlier period in history. Markets were rebuilt in this postwar era and the workforce in general expanded rapidly, as increased production and a growing population propelled the economy.

This is an interesting period in history in which to study how some very successful businesspeople anticipated consumer need, filled it, and rode the resulting wave of success.

As a result of this expanding economy, many of the early boomers (and those born just prior to the boom years) were able to choose a career and work for the same company or organization for most of their working life. Additionally, once an individual began working for a large company there were often many benefits to staying with that organization, such as health insurance, retirement packages, and savings plans for childrens' education. Companies expanded rather than downsized, and though work was a necessary fact of life, for most it was not the obsession that it has become for people today.

 The sheer numbers of boomers drive the economy with their needs. Please see Evaluating Opportunities for more details.

 "The highest reward for a person's toil is not what they get for it, but what they become by it."

—John Ruskin

Generation X

The baby boomers are the parents of the population group currently labeled "Generation X" whose members find themselves frustrated with choosing a career and with today's job market in general. These people are often caught in the trap of thinking their careers should go the way their parents' did, working at the same job for the same company for as many years as they want. Unfortunately, that work environment rarely exists for today's career seekers. Indeed, the definition of career has changed considerably between the boomer and the X generations.

 "The older you get, the more you like to tell it like it used to be."

—Anonymous

Remember, and remind yourself as often as you need to, if you are setting out to choose your first career, many of those boomer parents are not necessarily aware of how drastically the career market has changed in the last 15 or 20 years. As a result, they may not understand why their children cannot find a job or, if they do, why it is only a temporary or contract position. Know that your boomer parents and relatives mean well when they encourage you to find a "stable" job with a big company, one with a retirement plan and good benefits, but be aware that that type of career is the exception in today's job market, not the rule.

 When choosing a career, no matter what your age you will find people who cannot understand why you don't choose something that will "guarantee" you a lifetime job. Smile and thank those people for their input, then continue on with your realistic decision.

Which Leaves Us Where?

Well, it's the 1990s, and the pace of life seems to have quickened considerably. People are spending much more time on their education and are expecting suitable rewards for that time spent. Along with that, sadly, we have become a society generally consumed by the desire for material and technological wealth. Even more tragically, we often judge our happiness and the relative happiness of those around us by material wealth. We often assume those who have more things have more happiness.

 Be sure when choosing your career it is because it interests you and you feel you can achieve some good in it, not because you hear you can make a lot of money doing it.

It is quite normal and understandable that the parents in every generation want their children to have more than they did: more money, more advantages, more opportunities, more "things." We have reached the virtual peak of that cycle, however, and may be the last generation to have more than our parents did. The nature of society and careers is such that it is simply becoming impossible to earn more money any faster and, therefore, attitudes and values are slowly beginning to change.

 "If a man does not keep pace with his companions, perhaps it is because he hears a different drummer. Let him step to the music which he hears, however measured or far away."

—Henry David Thoreau

Today, because the nature of work and career has changed and continues to change, peoples' attitudes toward work and how it should fit into their lives will also have to evolve. Although people are aware the job market is increasingly competitive and that to excel in any field a job will devour more than 8 hours a day, 5 days a week, there is a slow realization that there should be more to life than work.

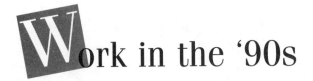 Work in the '90s

The very nature of work in the '90s itself demands that peoples' lives change. With more and more people finding contract, home-based, and small-business careers, or a combination of all of these, society will have to evolve accordingly. Diversity, flexibility, and a greater willingness to try new and different things: these are the key words and phrases of the career-minded individual of the nineties.

 Continually trying new things— whether hobbies or projects—will help give you the right frame of mind to keep your career changing and evolving with the times.

This is not to say that you will choose a career direction now and then have to head back to school every five years or so to completely retrain yourself for a new career. What it may mean, however, is that you will make your career choice now and that education or a particular set of skills and interests will be simply the outline of your career for as many years as you choose to work.

What is increasingly unlikely today is the notion that you will finish your training or education, find a job with a stable company, and spend the next 20 years there moving up the corporate ladder. Instead, your career will probably consist of shorter-term jobs or contract positions with large or small organizations, and perhaps at some time you will take the leap and start your own small business or even a home-based business. All of these jobs may be in the same industry or field, or they may simply be loosely related.

 As everyone must, you will have to keep your skills and training current, but it may not be necessary to completely change your educational background.

So it would seem that the history of "career," although not repeating itself exactly, is close to coming full circle. Even though a career will never be exactly what it was early in the century, we are slowly beginning to adopt some historical values when it comes to work and career and how they fit in our lives.

 If you ever find yourself depressed or frustrated by your quest for a suitable career, sit down and talk with your grandparents, if possible. You may find you are not so frustrated with your options as you think.

Obviously, there will never be the need for as many farmers or people to work the land as there once was. Technology has also replaced many people in mines, factories, and some large corporations, and because of a depletion of many types of resources, from fish to oil, there are reductions in the number of people in those industries. Additionally (don't get discouraged, there is a bright side to all of this), history will never, and can never, repeat itself exactly because of the drastic increases in world population and the technology we as a society have developed.

However, we are learning as a society that there is more to life than work and career. Slowly there is a return to time with family and time for self, away from the tendency to put all of that off until tomorrow in the quest for excessive financial gain or unrealistic career goals. We have a long way to go, but the trend is beginning.

 Regardless of this slow attitude evolution, there is still considerable pressure in society to make money and have nice things. Know for yourself when enough is enough. You must be able to define success. It is far too easy to find yourself caught in the "more money" cycle.

You'll find more on defining success in Chapter 2.

The Point

So what does all of this historical hoopla have to do with you?

Well, it is important that you understand what *career* means to you and that means:

- understanding what careers have been in the past and what they are becoming;

- knowing that people in a different age bracket than you may have a different view of what a career is and should be;

- being prepared in your lifetime to see the definition of career change again.

Career is a major force in any person's life, but it is not all there is to life. You must make it fit with your lifestyle, your goals, and, most importantly, your values. If you are not happy, comfortable, and confident with your career choice and how it shapes you and your life, it will create some obstacles.

Regardless of how you perceive your career and its importance in your life, it does have some social implications. Whether we mean for it to happen or not, the pressure of what other people think about what we "do" for a living has an effect on us. Imagine yourself in any social situation meeting people for the first time. How does the conversation usually go? "Hi, nice to meet you, Chris, what do you do?" If you are unsure of where your career is going, embarrassed or uncomfortable with what you do, or simply in a transition in your career, those moments can be unnecessarily stressful or awkward.

This DOES NOT mean you should choose a career that is trendy so you can entertain people with office anecdotes at parties! Choose your career realistically and honestly, with care and attention to who you are and what is important to you, and your life will be more than interesting enough to discuss at parties.

 Remember that simply due to the nature of the job market today there are many people unemployed, under-employed, self-employed, or in transition. Do not be embarrassed by where you are in your decision-making process.

Career by Definition

According to the *Oxford Dictionary*—

Career: Course or progress through life; course of professional life or employment; way of making livelihood.

Career: To move or run rapidly, as a horse or ship, etc.—also interesting, but totally irrelevant to this discussion!

According to *Webster's New Encyclopedic Dictionary*—

Career: A specific course of action or occupation forming the object of one's life.

**Please take note that neither defi-
nition includes the word stability!**

"Forming the object of one's life" sounds rather serious and could make you more than a little nervous about narrowing the field down to only one career choice. Relax... a bit. The *Webster* definition sounds a bit extreme and hopefully you are a well-rounded person with diverse interests and influences and there is more helping to form the object of your life than your career.

When you find yourself panicking about choosing a career, sit back and take a realistic look at your time line. There is no rule that states you must make this decision in a certain amount of time. Take a break if you need one.

Oxford's definition is perhaps more suited to the career of the '90s. "Course or progress through life" implies that you will spend some time charting and planning that course, but there will be times when you may simply be along for the ride and will follow the opportunities where they lead, open to new ideas and new direction. This is a much more healthy attitude and one that will leave you open for opportunity when it comes your way. You, of course, have control of your career and where you want to go. But remember that every now and again fate will throw something your way just to see if you are paying attention.

Try not to get caught in the trap of thinking you must make this career decision only once for the rest of your working life. Make your decision in pencil: there is always room for change.

Just remember, however, that being open to opportunity when it comes your way and not making a decision in the name of leaving yourself open to whatever comes your way are two totally different things. By not making a decision and trying to remain open to all options, you paralyze yourself and make a *real* decision—based on your hard work, goals, and values—impossible.

In order to create posibilities for yourself, you must have a direction, a focus, a game plan. If you don't, how on Earth can you be sure something is an opportunity and not simply a distraction? Your focus does not need to be written in stone, but it certainly should be a penciled-in map!

 "One falls to the ground in trying to sit between two stools."
—**Rabelais**

Changing Times

We certainly have determined that the '90s are a fast-paced work environment, one where you never know what will come your way and one where you can expect to change your career, or at least modify your direction, every five or so years. Is it sounding like nothing is really certain in your life? So how on Earth do you prepare for and deal with the constant changes that are happening around you and to you?

The first and most important step in dealing with change and the constant prospect of change is to:

1. Expect it
   and
2. Accept it.

What?

Yes, expect it. The most disarming and stressful fact of change is often the surprise of it. Change catches us off-guard, unprepared, and suddenly we find ourselves reeling under new circumstances. So, if you always keep in the back of your mind that change is inevitable, there are no surprises.

There is an old saying that the only constant in life is change, and it has never been more true than today. If you find yourself in what you think is a comfortable, stable job, congratulations. If you are planning your life around the notion that you will be in that same comfortable, stable job for as long as you want, you could be setting yourself up for some unnecessary stress.

Not only will you find you may miss out on opportunities that present themselves because you don't want to take any risks, but one of two other things also may happen:

1. You will work away happily in your job:

    • not making contingency plans

    • not having planned for changes in your career

    • not keeping your eyes and ears open for additional opportunities

    And you may suddenly, one day, lose your job. The stress of change will hit you full force, which can be devastating.

2. You will not work away happily in ignorant bliss in your job. Instead, you know your job will probably not last forever, yet you fail, out of fear of change, to plan for anything different. As a result, you find yourself:

    • listening to unfounded office gossip about possible layoffs

    • spending more time worrying about whether you'll be working tomorrow than you do working today

    • losing sleep and spoiling your free time with stress you bring home from work

    • feeling generally unhappy

    Again, the threat and stress of change wins again.

 Be optimistic about the possibilities that exist for you. You will be surprised at how your positive attitude aids your career decisions now and your willingness to change.

Change is inevitable: accept it when it happens. Often we find ourselves fighting change in our life because we are unsure if we can handle it. If you take the energy that it takes to work against the changing factors in your life and put it toward investigating where these new circumstances may take you, you may suddenly discover that what you thought to be a devastating, stress-filled change is really a challenging opportunity.

"Start planning your second career while you're still on your first one."

—David Brown

Preparing for Change

Granted, this all sounds very easy when you read it on paper. It is completely different when you are in the midst of a career crisis. Although your attitude toward change is the most important factor in dealing with it, there are a few other ways to prepare yourself.

How?

1. Practice change:

   Make it a regular habit to shake up your routine. This can mean little things or sometimes, just for fun, the big things.

   - Try drying yourself off differently when you get out of the shower. (Yes, it sounds ridiculous, but the next few times you get out of the shower, pay attention to how you dry yourself off. See if it's the same each time and, if it is, change it. You may be surprised how difficult this habit is to break!

   - If you always sleep on the same side of the bed, change.

   - Take a different route to work.

   - Be spontaneous and take a last-minute, unplanned weekend away (if budgets permit).

   - Have toast in the morning occasionally instead of always having cereal!

   Whatever it is, big or small, you determine the stakes, take a risk, and change your comfortable routine now and again. You will quickly learn to trust yourself. You will not fall apart when presented with something new, you will learn something about yourself, you might laugh a little, your life might become a little more interesting, and you may even discover you enjoy "shakin' it up" now and again!!

2. Create something stable in your life:

If you have accepted the fact that your job is not a sure thing and you know your employment status will evolve with the changing economy—great. Realistically, however, over time you may find stress building in your life simply because you feel as though nothing is ever for sure. Create something.

You may be surprised how calming it is to know that once a week you will meet a friend for a game of squash, for example. It isn't a big thing, but it is a consistent thing. Much as we try to deny it, we are to a degree creatures of habit, and it is not a bad thing to have something we can call our own, something we do regularly for ourselves.

 It is a great idea to make this "regular thing" a physical activity of some kind. Not only does it give you something to look forward to, the physical activity itself is a great stress reliever.

3. Be aware of things changing around you:

Once again, the most likely time change will be devastating for you is when it sneaks up on you and catches you unaware and unprepared. If you make it a habit to be aware of…

- changes in the job market that are going on around you,
- changes in technology that may affect your industry,
- changes in company hiring policies that may affect your employment,
- any opportunities that may be a direction your career could take

… you can take the "sneak" out of any attack change may make on your life!

4. Do not rely on your job to fulfill your every need:

If work is all you do and suddenly, for whatever reason, you lost your job, what would you do? If the answer to that is you don't know, or you would have nothing to fill your time, you need to make some changes in your life.

There is a distinct possibility that you will change your career at some point in your life. In those in-between times it is essential to your peace of mind to have other interests and other areas of support rather than simply your job. Develop those areas now. Remember, "all work and no play made Jack a very dull boy!"

5. Be aware of your strengths and weaknesses:

   Undoubtedly, change will have some effect on you, so be prepared for that. Know what your personal strengths are and also who are the people in your life you can turn to for support.

   Equally important, know your weaknesses. If you know how stress tends to affect you, you can be prepared for it. Pay attention to how you react in stressful situations. Sometimes your symptoms—be they overeating, not sleeping, or sleeping too much—inform you that you are under stress before your brain does.

   There really is nothing that can prepare you completely for all the changes you will experience in your life, neither the big ones nor the small ones. But practicing these ideas, coupled with expecting and accepting change, can take the unnecessary stress out of change.

Remember, all stress is not bad. Stress in moderation helps us take on greater challenges in life and grow as individuals.

Opportunities in Disguise

"Turbulence is life force. It is opportunity. Let's love turbulence and use it for a change."

—Ramsay Clark

It is a somewhat frightening prospect to be setting out to choose your career, putting in all the necessary time and considerable effort, only to have in the back of your mind… "I may very possibly have to do this again four more times!"

Fear not!

Once you begin the process and launch happily into your career, you will find it much easier to streamline it with your changing needs and values. As you work away in your chosen field you may be given the opportunity to explore different avenues of that particular industry.

 Always be willing to try new things to expand your horizons. When colleagues or friends ask you to participate in activities or events, try to make a habit of saying "yes."

Additionally, you will meet people who have been in "the business" for a number of years with more insight than you, and they will help you shape your choices and decide what you want to do as your career develops and grows. Just as important, these people may illustrate for you the things you do *not* want to do or become. This is how careers evolve.

Another Change?

It is, in fact, somewhat misleading to say you will *change* careers a number of times in your lifetime. The correct statement should perhaps be: your career will evolve considerably as you continue to work. Certainly, though, you may experience some radical career moves because of any number of circumstances. Remember, many of these circumstances, though unwelcome, stress-filled, and uncontrollable, may be opportunities in disguise.

How?

• Your health may change and require you to change professions.

Often times a change in your health is your body's way of telling you you are asking too much of it, or there is simply too much stress in your life. Making a career change may very well improve your health, your well-being, and, as a result, your happiness.

- The industry in which you are employed may become obsolete.

Perhaps your industry becoming obsolete will force you to go back to school, update your education, and increase both your marketability and your earning potential.

- The company where you have worked for years may close down.

Perhaps if you really thought about it you would realize and be able to admit that actually you were not happy in your job. Now may be the time to use some of your industry contacts to explore your options and move laterally into a new area of the same type of work.

- Your spouse has got a fabulous promotion but it means moving to a new city.

If you do some research you may find the company you work with has sister organizations in the new city, or perhaps they are looking to expand. If the sort of work you do allows it, you may even be able, with advances in the available technology, to work long-distance on a contract basis with your current employer.

 Opportunity does present itself in the most unusual ways. Do not be too quick to judge any situation. You may be surprised at the opportunity it presents.

- You and your spouse have decided to have a child, and you would prefer one of you stay home rather than place the child in daycare. You make less money—you should be the one to quit your job.

Wanting to stay home with your new child may also be the time to slowly start researching and trying your own home-based business.

- Tragic circumstances may occur that require you to assume responsibilities you would not normally have.

Certainly this is not an easy situation. If you are forced to take time from your career to deal with any personal tragedy, it may also be a valuable time to evaluate yourself, your needs, your values, and your career and decide if you are happy or satisfied with the direction in which you are going.

All of these situations may seem inopportune at the time and you may feel they have put an unnecessary glitch in your life. Make it your practice to look for the opportunity in disguise, the diamond in the rough! You may find something you couldn't have planned better yourself!

As average human beings we are all creatures of comfort and creatures of habit to varying degrees. So what? Well, this translates into the fact that we all get comfortable in and with our situations and surroundings, and change becomes increasingly difficult as the years go by. When one of these changes slaps us in the face, it may seem horrible at the time but such changes can be good "rut busters!" We all get stuck in a rut at least once in our career. Sometimes it takes a little push to get us out and sometimes it takes an Earth-moving event. Either way, once you get over the initial shock, try to find the good in your new circumstances. Change is healthy. Accept it and grow with it!

 "People wish to learn to swim and at the same time to keep one foot on the ground."

—Marcel Proust

 **C**ontract Work

Consider:

Many people who once had full-time, "stable" jobs have lost their steady employment to budget cuts and company streamlining. Although this seems like only bad news, there is an upside to it as well. Many companies that find themselves downsizing will find the company cannot function with fewer employees. As a result, the company may have to hire employees back on a contract basis.

Why?

Money. It is often cheaper to pay a contract employee an increased hourly or daily rate than it is to have that person as a full-time employee making less money. Make sense? No, it doesn't, until you look at the amount of money companies spend on benefit packages, retirement and savings plans for employees, additional employee training, and company perks from fitness passes to expense accounts. When a company eliminates full-time employees and hires them back as contract workers, the company is no longer obligated to provide any of those additional employee perks. The result? The company can afford to pay a slightly higher rate to contract workers and save themselves money in the long run.

 If you find yourself the victim of a layoff, make it known to your employer you are flexible enough with your career to take on some contract work. You never know where it may lead.

Additionally, the company is not obligated to keep contract workers employed, nor give them extended notice or buyouts when a position is terminated. A contract employee is hired usually on the basis of a particular project and when that project is complete, so is the term of employment. Simple and cost-effective.

Even from an administrative perspective, it is easier for a company to employ contract workers. When a person is a full-time employee of a company, that organization is responsible for deducting various taxes from each employee's pay, possibly making retirement savings contributions on that employee's behalf, and maybe even having to calculate shared company/employee savings plans. As a contract worker, you become responsible for all of these. An employer simply writes you a check for services rendered and you are required to give the government its share, but you can put your money wherever you want! This undoubtedly increases further the incentives for a company to rehire you as a contract worker.

Unfortunately, it is not guaranteed that a company will rehire people on a contract basis after layoffs. It never hurts to ask, though.

So, we find ourselves at the turn of a new century with a job market that resembles the job market at this century's beginning—a market in which people did not have the same job forever. Rather, people had to be diverse to cope with changing needs, changing seasons, and most definitely a changing economy. Adaptability is indeed the key to success today as it was then.

Be aware of this and prepare yourself for some exciting, challenging change!

How'd They Get There?
Adrian Paul

Adrian Paul is the star and sometimes director of television's "Highlander: The Series."

Growing up in England, Adrian never made a conscious, researched decision to make acting his career. Rather, he pursued his interest in sports, playing semipro soccer for a number of years, and dance, working as a professional dancer and choreographer, all the while working to create new opportunities for himself.

As a man who always tries to live his life open to new opportunities, experiences, and directions, Adrian followed that spirit of adventure to New York to model with Ford Model. From there, it wasn't long before he moved to Los Angeles to act. Although Adrian didn't have considerable previous experience, once he began acting on camera, he knew he had found his niche.

When Adrian isn't working, he's studying, always striving to expand and perfect his trade. He still finds himself looking for new avenues to explore and when it comes to trying new career directions he listens to his instincts to keep him on track.

Although he knows nothing is ever guaranteed, Adrian is confident that through consistent hard work and perseverance, new opportunities will continue to arise and he will be as successful as he wants to be.

The Road to Success

Success is a goal for many people and this goal often influences the choices we make. Choosing a career in which you will excel is important to your overall sense of self. Choose your career wisely and you will be challenged and stimulated forever.

"Strong lives are motivated by dynamic purposes."

—Kenneth Hildebrand

Planning for Success

Before deciding which careers could make you successful, take a look at what success is. Will you be successful after you make your first million? Billion? Does providing for your family make you a success? Is a successful person the one who rises through the ranks of the company or do your parents have to say "I'm proud of you" before you believe that you have arrived at the end of the road to success? Is there an end to the road to success?

Your view of success will differ from other people's, but it is important to look at what being successful means to you. Take the time to consider this and write your definition of success. Include the things you feel you must do or accomplish to be a success.

I will be successful when:

_____

_____

_____

_____

_____

_____

Far be it for us to tell you what success is, but here are some thoughts on the subject.

Consider:

When Barry was 21 he knew what he wanted out of life: to find a career, move up through the ranks to management, and have enough money to retire by the age of 60.

He did it!

Is Barry a success?

Barry encountered a few glitches along the way that made the road of life seem more like gravel than pavement. Barry married, had three children, a dog, and, after 15 years of constant work, divorce papers. He had been transferred to several different cities so he didn't have any close friends. Barry was recently diagnosed with a stress-related illness, which will affect him for the rest of his life.

Is Barry a success?

If Barry truly believed that success meant attaining an end result, for example, retiring at 60, then maybe he would be successful. But it seems there is more to success than simply reaching a goal.

The way we reach our goals, and the feelings and emotions associated with what we do, affects how successful we feel. Our emotions have a significant impact on our feelings of success.

Judging Success

Before we go any further, think about people you know (not people you know *of*, but people you really *know*) and write the names of those who you think are successful. Identify why you believe they are successful.

Who is successful?	Why are they successful?
_____	_____
	_____
	_____
	_____
	_____
_____	_____
	_____
	_____
	_____
_____	_____
	_____
	_____
	_____

Look at the reasons you identified. Chances are that a few of the reasons have something to do with the people being happy, enjoying what they do, or feeling content with their lives. The feeling of fulfillment is very important when considering whether or not a person is a success.

 Success is affected by our feelings of happiness, contentment, and fulfillment.

This exercise should help you to identify that there is more to success than simply meeting a goal. It also, unfortunately, demonstrates how easy it is to judge other people. It is tempting, and common, to use your own criteria and values to determine another person's success in life. You might take ten seconds to evaluate another person's entire life and then label them. You might judge their success based on whether or not they meet *your* criteria for success and not their own.

Consider

1. Lee is a university graduate who began her career as a social worker. After working hard under stressful conditions for two years and enduring a three-week-long strike, she quit her job. Four months later, she was hired in a six month temporary research position. After another brief period of unemployment, she was hired as a workshop facilitator, where she worked for two years. Lee then became pregnant and is now staying home with her two children.

   Is Lee a success?

2. Brendan began working immediately after graduating from high school. He had various jobs, ranging from working as a plumber and electrical assistant with his uncles, to operating a backhoe for a railroad company. He finally got a permanent job as a laborer with a large fertilizer company. Brendan has been there for 14 years, is working shifts, and has had one job promotion.

   Is Brendan a success?

 "When people are bored, it is primarily with their own selves that they are bored."
   —Eric Hoffer

3. Devin's family owns a medium-sized business where he began working after completing his college education. He started at ground level, moved up through the ranks quickly, and is now a partner in the company. He earns a good salary, has considerable responsibility, and will inherit part of the business upon his father's retirement.

   Is Devin a success?

   Now that you have considered how successful these people are, take a look at what they think.

1. Lee considers herself to be a success. She enjoyed all the jobs she had and each career change was her choice. She now finds being a full-time mother to be the most rewarding part of her career thus far. Lee would not change a decision or a day in her life.

2. Brendan makes enough money to pay for the sporting activities he is passionate about. The shift work allows him time for both his hobbies and his family. Brendan finds his life very fulfilling.

Your strength lies in who you are, not in what you do.

3. While Devin has all the material things and power he could want, he is very unhappy. Devin works a considerable amount of overtime and feels he is losing touch with his family. He has no hobbies, time for sports, and longs for a less demanding job.

What appears to be good or bad from the outside often shows itself in a different light when looked at from the inside. How you perceive others can be considerably different from how they perceive themselves.

Ask people you know if they feel they are successful. Ask why or why not, and listen to what they say.

Judging Yourself

So you understand that someone else may view his or her success differently than you would, but how does this affect you? Simply put, how we live our lives is determined by our thoughts, beliefs, and self-confidence. And how we see ourselves is often influenced by how others see us. Therefore, how others see us can affect how we see ourselves. This is a scary thought, but unfortunately it is often true.

"What a man thinks of himself, that it is which determines or rather indicates his fate."

—Henry David Thoreau

Research has shown that children who are continuously told they are bad begin to believe it and act more "bad." On the other hand, children who are encouraged and told the things they do are good develop a more positive self-image. If this is true for children, why not for adults?

Consider:

Cameron enjoys theater and has been pursuing a career in acting. He has been in a few productions, enjoyed them immensely, and is very happy with his work. However, because the acting jobs come sporadically and don't pay very well, he is living on the bare minimum.

Cameron's family wonders how he can live this way. They call frequently to find out how he is doing and even on occasion tell him about jobs they have lined up... if only he would come home and settle down. The first time this happened, Cameron was offended, but over time he has begun to question whether his family is right and if he would be happier with a steady income.

Cameron's opinion of his life has been changing because of what others think.

"The great man is he who does not lose his child's heart."

—Mencius

It is hard not to be influenced by other people, but the next time someone seems to be judging your life, ask yourself these questions:

- Are you really happy with what you are doing? If you are, remind yourself of this: it is what *you* want that really matters.

Think about why you are happy with your life and write the reasons down. If people imply that you must be unhappy, tell them you are not and why.

- Think about how happy the other person is with her life. Could it be she is envious of the pleasure you find in what you are doing? Don't take on someone else's misery as your own.

People who are unhappy often try to make others feel as terrible as they do. Instead of letting others' bad feelings be contagious, concentrate on the good feelings you have. Maybe your good feelings will rub off on them.

- Will you really be happier doing something else? If you trade a passion for a steady paycheck, will you regret your decision?

"To go against one's conscience is neither safe nor right. Here I stand. I cannot do otherwise."

—Martin Luther

- Can you try something new and—if you don't like it—return to what you were doing before? If so, then the decision isn't as ominous as you may have thought. You can always go back.

Remember that other people's opinions are just that, *their* opinions. Don't take them on as your own.

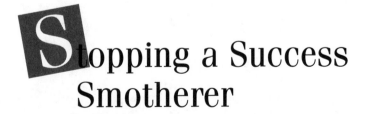

Stopping a Success Smotherer

Sometimes it seems people are out to rain on your parade and find fault in the things you do. While they can influence what you think of yourself if you allow it, there are things you can do to help maintain an "attitude of success."

When people try to smother your success—or if you find you cave in to thoughts of "lessness" rather than thoughts of greatness—combat them with one of these:

✔ When people ask you what type of work you do, never say "I am *just a... .*" You are important whether you are a lawyer, ditchdigger, computer programmer, seamstress, stay-at-home parent, or whatever. Whatever you do there is value, worth, and importance in it.

 Write down the things you enjoy about the work you do. Whenever you feel your work has little value, read this list to remind yourself of its importance.

✔ If you currently aren't working, don't tell people "I used to be a...." This implies that you now do nothing and, very likely, this is not true. If you are looking for work, say "I am a... looking for employment" or "I am retired and now do...." The things you do now, work or not, are of value and importance to you.

✔ Never say "I can't...." *Can't* is a debilitating word that allows you to give up trying and undermines your sense of strength and self. Instead say "I don't want to...," "I'll try later...," or "I choose not to...." You now have the choice to try later, and you still may do it. Take responsibility for wherever you are in your life. You have made the choice to be there.

 "Every noble work is at first impossible."

—Thomas Carlyle

✔ When people ask "What do you do?" focus on the things that make you truly happy. This could be your career, your family life, a sport, or a hobby. True success comes from the things that make you happy: describe these first.

✔ When someone tells you "You can't do that…," decide for yourself if it is possible. Never let someone else determine your direction for you.

"He was a *how* thinker, not an *if* thinker."

—Anonymous

✔ When making decisions, make them based on your thoughts, not on what others will think. It's your life, you have to live it.

✔ When faced with a challenge, look at it as an opportunity rather than a barrier. Change your "why me's" to "thank you for giving me this opportunity to prove what I can do."

"Adversity causes some people to break; others to break records."

—William A. Ward

Attitudes are the biggest barriers to success. If you look at the things you say and do, and make them more positive, you may be surprised by how much better you feel about yourself.

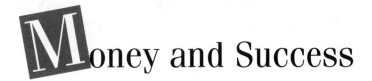Money and Success

Money is a necessity in today's society, and it is essential to think about it. When choosing a career, you must decide if it will provide you with enough money to meet your needs and provide extra for things you want. You may not be very happy eating hamburger if you thought you would be able to afford lobster.

However, and this is a huge however, don't forget the other things in life that are important.

"For of all sad words of tongues or pen the saddest are these: It might have been."

—John Greenleaf Whittier

In the fast-paced, competitive, money-oriented society of today, many of the "old values" and morals have been put aside. People complete tasks for the rewards they will receive, rather than for the inner satisfaction it will provide. As children we did chores; not to create a tidy home, but to get paid. We carried the elderly neighbor's groceries; not to be kind and generous, but to get paid. Now we work; not for the enjoyment of it, but to get paid. "If I do…, then I will get…" is our rationale for doing many things. And we often judge our success by the size of our paycheck.

But is life really about how much money you make, or is there more to it than that?

Consider:

✔ You will be spending approximately half your waking hours at work. If you are only there for the money, how fulfilling will your life be?

✔ How important are your family and friends? People who focus on money sometimes put family and friends second, and thus lose them. Decide early where your priorities lie.

Ask elderly friends or family what they feel the important things in life are. Listen and learn from the wisdom of experience.

✔ Consider life after work. What do you want to do when you retire? People who spend their entire lives focusing on money often forget to enjoy the fruits of their labors.

Instead of waiting until you retire to do the things you enjoy, begin now. When you retire you will already know how to lead the life you want and it won't be such a huge adjustment. And if you should die before you retire, you will have done the things that are important to you.

✔ If you were to die next year, how would you want to be remembered? Remember the old cliche: "Money can't buy happiness."

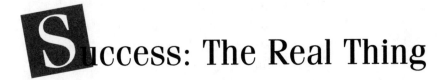

Success: The Real Thing

So, we've looked at the illusion of success. Now it's time to look at what success really is. Discover what it takes to have a career that is rewarding and satisfying, and that fits with the rest of your life.

"My mother said to me, 'If you become a soldier you'll be a general; if you become a monk you'll end up as the pope.' Instead, I became a painter and wound up as Picasso."

—Pablo Picasso

Success Is a Process

Success is a process that can be compared to a vacation.

Some vacationers are *planners* who coordinate every part of their trip, leaving nothing to chance. They plan their route, monitor the weather, pack everything they could possibly need, and then (if the stars are aligned properly) set out on their trip. They drive directly to their destination, follow the itinerary to a tee, and, once all the "things to do" have been done, they leave for home. Anything that was not planned causes them to hit the panic button and begin frantically rescheduling.

"Sit loosely in the saddle of life."

—Robert Louis Stevenson

Spontaneous vacationers make no plans at all and may not even know where they are going until they get there. They make last-minute decisions, pack right before they leave, and hope that everything will fall into place. They go to the attractions they happen to hear about but miss out on much because they didn't know what was available. After the trip is over they swear they will be more prepared next time.

Flexible vacationers know where they are going and have tentative plans but are flexible enough to go with the flow. They stop to enjoy the sights along the way and find getting to their destination to be as much fun as the destination itself. The trip home isn't an ending, but is also part of the vacation and fun.

Success for many people is like one of these vacations.

Like the *planner*, some people approach their careers by planning for and working toward goals. They do anything they can to achieve these goals, and forget to "enjoy the trip." They are so busy trying to be successful, they forget their lives are passing them by. When they attain "success," they'll "check off" rather than enjoy this brief moment, and then identify and work toward the next goal.

Or, like the *spontaneous vacationer*, there are those who make no plans for a career and things just happen. While these people can easily "go with the flow," they tend to look back on their careers and see there was a lot they could have done. They enjoy what they do but see many opportunities they missed. If they could relive their career, they would make more conscious, informed career decisions.

"Keep strong if possible; in any case keep cool."

—Sir Basil Liddell Hart

Flexible planners know where they are going and remember to enjoy the journey. They enjoy the everyday tasks and make time to try out new things. They allow themselves to take temporary detours along their career paths to keep them interesting and rewarding. When they achieve their goals they enjoy the benefits, but don't see this success as an ending. The time after is cherished and experienced as well.

The key to a successful career is to enjoy it *all*. Enjoy setting your goals, enjoy the things you do each day in pursuit of these goals, enjoy the "time at the top," and enjoy the time afterwards. If you take your career one step at a time and find value in each step, then success will be yours, always. You will feel successful all the way.

 ## Success is not an event. It is a lifestyle.

Each step you take makes you as much of a success as does reaching your goals.

Success Is Attitude

 ## "We are what we believe we are."
—Benjamin N. Cardozo

Have you ever looked at a person, wished you had what they did, and then heard them complain about the things they don't have? If only they saw how little you had, maybe they would be happier….
Maybe someone is looking at you and saying the same thing.

 ## "Nothing can bring you peace but yourself."
—Ralph Waldo Emerson

It is up to you to decide how you will view your career. If you choose to focus on the positive things you will be happier and feel more successful. If you concentrate on things that go wrong, you will probably wait a long time before you feel good about the work you do.

Every career and every job has its good and bad points. Concentrate on the things that work and make you feel good. Focus on the positive aspects of your career and life and you will feel more successful.

 Each night, write down five things you enjoyed about the day. This will help you to focus on the positive things.

Along with appreciating what is good, take responsibility for the things you don't like. If you have a hard time finding positive things to say about the work you do, then it is up to you to change your approach to work or change the work you do. If you can't find good in what you do, then change what you do.

 The good things of life are not to be had singly but come to us with a mixture.

—Charles Lamb

By appreciating what you do like and changing the things you don't, you take control of your life and make your career one worth having. *You* make your career, so make it what you want.

Success Is More than Work

Success is something much more than accomplishments and achievements at work. Success is about doing things that make you happy, proud, satisfied, and fulfilled. *You are more than the work you do*, and the various aspects of your life contribute to making you a success.

The following is a list of things that may be important to you. By taking a conscious look at the things of value in your life, you will be more likely to make time for them, thus making sure they remain important.

 Refer to this values list often. It will help you to keep things in perspective.

Identify whether these things are very important, somewhat important, or not important to you.

Relationship with:

best friends

casual acquaintances

mother

father

sisters

brothers

spouse

children

pets

grandparents

co-workers

aunts

uncles

cousins

God

"People before things."

—La Leche League International

Time spent on:

relationships

hobbies

sports

reading

learning

self-development

socializing

thinking

"There is no happiness in having or in getting, but only in giving."

—Henry Drummond

Things you have:

    money

    house

    vehicles

    clothes

    household items

    tools

    hobby items

    sporting equipment

    club memberships

    other items (please identify)

Remember the things that are important to you, and always make time for them. Your career may have a significant impact on how successful you feel, but it is not the *only* influence.

Your personal life and the things you do outside of work are at least as important as the things you do at work. Make time for them, too.

Consider not only your career, but all parts of your life, in your quest for success. Material goods or how others rate your life are not what matter. It is whether or not you find value in what you do that determines how successful you are. Work hard in *all* areas of your life and you will feel complete and satisfied.

Our Life is what our thoughts make of it.

—**Marcus Aurelius**

Success Is You

Your views of success may have changed since beginning this chapter. Recognize that there is no one right definition; in fact, there are more ways to define success than there are people. You may even find that you redefine success at different times in your life.

As you mature and grow, you will discover new things about yourself, your abilities, and your perspective, all of which can change how you view success.

Your career will not be the only aspect of your life that makes you successful. All of the following components can also add to your feelings of success:

✔ how you live your life

✔ what you do with your leisure time

✔ how you react to other people and how they react to you

✔ how you raise your children

✔ how you view the world

✔ how much satisfaction you gain

Now it's time to define what success is for *you*. Consider all the components of success listed above.

The following are different elements that you may include in your success formula. Use the ones that are good for you, forget the ones you can't relate to, and add any others you value.

✔ Happiness

✔ Fulfillment

✔ Enjoyment

✔ Living passionately

✔ Providing joy to others

✔ Finding joy

✔ Valuing what you do

✔ Enthusiasm

✔ Making a difference

What success means to me:

_____

_____

_____

_____

_____

Discovering success is your responsibility. No one else can find it for you or help you get there. Look for success in everything you do and you will find your career and life to be everything you could want.

 "He did it with all his heart, and prospered."

2 Chronicles 31:24

How'd They Get There?
Jean Pare

Jean Pare is the author of the *Company's Coming* cookbooks. She has written 30 books and sold over 11 million copies. Her books are distributed worldwide and have been translated into French and Spanish.

So, how did Jean get there?

Jean began cooking and baking at home as a child. She waited on customers in her parents' store (receiving no pay) before beginning a family of her own. A full-time mother of four children, Jean also managed a coffee shop, worked in the office, and balanced the books for two auction houses.

Her life took a turn when she offered to cater a function for over 1,000 people; soon after Jean began a catering business. People constantly asked Jean for recipes and even suggested that she publish a cookbook. Jean, having an eye for opportunity, did exactly that and within a week of releasing her first book no longer had time for her catering business!

Jean continues to write cookbooks and is awaiting the release of her first coffee-table book. She has expanded her business to include a sister company consisting of various café corporations, a publishing company, and a restaurant chain.

Jean feels that persistence, lots of hard work, and enjoying what she does have been the keys to her continued success.

Discovering Yourself

You are an individual unique from everyone else in the entire world. You have your own skills, interests, likes and dislikes, and they will influence the career choices you make and the lifestyle you choose. It is through discovering yourself that you will find the right career.

"Every man's work, whether it be literature, or music, or pictures, or architecture, or anything else, is always a portrait of himself."

—Samuel Butler

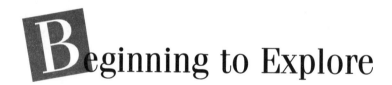

Beginning to Explore

Discovering who you are, what you are interested in, and the careers that excite you is a great adventure. It encourages you to look deep within yourself. It tugs at you to try new activities and explore different aspects of yourself. This is an exciting time in your life.

"The unexamined life is not worth living."

—Plato

For many people, however, this process can also be scary. Exploring deep within ourselves and discovering the multitude of career options can be intimidating and overwhelming. We often rationalize why we don't need to do it and contrive reasons for staying with the familiar and choosing careers that are "traditional" or "make sense." Often, we hesitate to explore the world of unknown careers because we don't know the answers to some important questions:

What will the future hold?

Who will I become?

What if my family and friends don't approve of my career choice?

What will happen if I make the wrong choice?

What if things don't turn out?

No one ever knows exactly what the future holds or how things will turn out in any situation. The best you can do is to make as good a choice as possible. The future is never stable or predictable and we must all do the best we can with what we have.

 "He who has a firm will molds the world to himself."

—Johann Wolfgang von Goethe

 aking Risks

Trying things that are "different" or unknown allows us to experience and discover new and unknown aspects of ourselves. We learn more, experience more, and live more. And this is good for everyone.

If you normally watch one type of movie (for example, action or comedy) try watching a movie of a different sort (for example, drama). You may discover that your interests are more diverse than you thought or that you really do have a passion for a specific type of movie. Either way, you have learned something about yourself.

How to begin?

Start with small steps and work into bigger ones.

First, encourage yourself to do things slightly differently.
Change things where there are no risks involved just to get used to doing things a different way. Buy a different brand of toothpaste; take a new route to the grocery store. Discover how wonderful new ideas and new ways of doing things can be.

Next, take small risks.
Ask a question you normally would keep to yourself or say "hello" to a stranger. Encourage yourself to be bold and take small risks so you get used to the feelings associated with doing these things.

 The first time you take a small risk you may find you have butterflies in your stomach. As you become more experienced at changing the way you do things, you will find the butterfly feeling is less intense and the butterflies start to fly in formation!

Finally, confront big risks.

Once you are comfortable taking small and medium risks it's time to consider taking larger ones… like choosing a career.

 The task of choosing a career will be easier to approach and less intimidating if you are comfortable dealing with small changes in your life.

Choosing a career can be "risky business," but it can be fun and exciting as well. By being open to new ideas and exploring alternatives, you allow yourself to experience the wonder and excitement of your career options.

 "Nothing in life is more exciting and rewarding than the sudden flash of insight that leaves you a changed person—not only changed, but for the better."

—Arthur Gordon

Choose a Career, Don't Fall into It

Your career is the work you will do during your life. This does not necessarily mean you will be doing the same job, but that your jobs will follow a unique path…your career. *You* must make this path one you want to follow.

"The destiny of man is in his own soul."

—Herodotus

Rather than leaving it to fate to determine the line of work you will do, *choose* a career that will make you successful by your own definition. Make conscious choices and decide what you want from a career. If you take control of your life and become responsible for the positions you hold, you greatly improve the chances of having a fulfilling career.

The World and All That Awaits

As you begin considering your career, realize that virtually the whole world is open to you. You have as many options as there are careers. The alternatives are endless. This is an exciting time of opportunity for you, when you can become anything you want.

Don't jump into things and decide on a career right away; take the time to think about all you can be and explore the world. Now is a time of adventure, a time to explore new worlds and careers. Enjoy the multitude of options that exist.

The word "can't" is a debilitating word and one you should try to eliminate from your vocabulary. Think instead about what you can do to make things possible.

Go on your own mental "walkabout" of the world. Learn and discover more about the world and what happens in it.

Begin by:

• reading magazine articles on topics you know nothing about,

• watching television documentaries about issues you have little knowledge of,

• speaking to people about jobs you are unfamiliar with,

- reading literature on businesses you have never heard of,

- doing anything else that piques your interest and expands your knowledge of careers and of the world.

By doing this you will begin to see how numerous career opportunities are. And your world will expand like never before.

"The great thing in this world is not so much where we are, but in what direction we are moving."

—Oliver Wendell Holmes

Too Many Choices

With constant developments in technology, greater diversity of businesses and occupations, and increasing global markets, you really are lucky to have so many career choices, right?

Maybe!

Having too many choices can be as paralyzing as having no choices at all. It may feel like you are in a room with a hundred doors to choose from, but you don't know which one to walk through. Any one of them could be the right one, but many of them could also be wrong. It is your approach and attitude that will determine how you face this sort of challenge.

One Approach:

One way to approach it is to sit down and not make any decisions, but to wait for a decision to be made for you, wait for someone else to open a door and invite you in. Then you walk through assuming the other person has made a decision that will be good for you, that what is beyond the door is what you want. This may or may not be the case.

Similarly, if you wait for someone else to tell you which career to choose, you may not be happy with what you get. Maybe a well-meaning family member finds you a job, brings you into the family business, chooses the college you will attend, or tells you outright which career to choose. Granted, it will be easy to complain and you will always have someone to blame if your career isn't exactly what you want, but will you be happy?

Even if the decision is a good one, if you haven't looked at the options and discovered things about yourself you may always wonder if there is something better out there. Never blindly walk into a career hoping it will be good for you. Choose your career yourself.

 Pressure from family, friends, guidance counselors, and others can make you feel your career decision has already been made. Before following through on other people's suggestions, do your own research to be sure the career you get into is one you will like. The motivation for a career should come from within you, not from someone else.

Second Approach:

Another alternative is to choose a door in a "game show" style. Close your eyes, spin around, pick a door and walk in. Then open your eyes and see what awaits you.

If you do this with your career—just take the first job that comes up or apply for the first job you see advertised—you really don't know what you are getting yourself into. Will you like what you are doing? Are you interested in this field? What opportunities have you passed up because of your rash decision?

Granted, you will be employed, and you may luck into a job that really interests you, but the downside is you may *not*. While conducting your career search in this manner will provide you with opportunities to work and try out different fields, you may never acquire a sense of direction that motivates and stimulates you.

And the worst part of this scenario is that if you don't like the job you get, you will have no one to blame for the decision. You chose the door, ill-informed as your choice may have been.

"Make the most of yourself, for that is all there is to you."

—Ralph Waldo Emerson

Third Approach:

A better alternative is to find out as much as you can about what is behind the doors, consider the information, and then make your choice. You may not know what lies behind each and every door, but you will have information on enough doors to make a good choice.

This is how choosing a career can be. Find out as much as you can about a variety of careers. Remember that you can never know everything about every career, but it is your responsibility to know as much as you can before making a decision. Then consider how each career would fit with your outlook and whether or not you would be happy. Don't stop searching until you find several careers that could be good for you. Finally, pick a career and follow through on it.

There are many career choices that could be good for you. It is not important to find the "perfect" career, but rather to find one that will be good for you and will make you happy. There will always be other things you could have done, but the key is in enjoying what you choose.

A well-informed decision that feels right is the best kind of decision there is.

"Take calculated risks. That is quite different from being rash."

—George S. Patton

Dream

Your head may swirl with everything you are learning and you may begin to see that there are many more careers than you had originally thought. You could be a cook, a missionary, a robotics technician, or a label designer. You can work with your hands, or with your thoughts. You can work with people, for people, or because of people, or you can work completely independently in your own home. You can do almost anything.

The next thing to do is to DREAM! Find a comfortable, quiet place and go there. Take all the excitement you have gathered from discovering your career options and use this to dream about your future. Fantasize about what you would do if there were no limitations, no responsibilities, no time or money worries. What would you do if you could do and be anything in the world?

Let your mind wander and explore all the things you have ever thought about doing. Dream about careers you have discovered that sound interesting and the jobs you think would be fun to try. Go where your mind takes you and dream about what the perfect career would be. Go into your dreamworld and fantasize.

 Take as much time as you need to dream. Enjoy the time you spend in your dream world and hold on to those feelings for a while.

DREAM NOW!

 "A man is what he thinks about all day long."

—Ralph Waldo Emerson

When you return from your dreamworld it's time to consider the careers you fantasized about. You may have thought of several careers that entice and thrill you, or you may have only one or two.

Either way, write down all your dream careers... and *never* forget them.

Work with Your Dreams

Your dreams may provide the key to discovering your career path. Many times all it takes is a good look at ourselves and our dreams to decide on the direction we will take. Look at your dream careers and begin to believe that they aren't merely fantasies, but possibilities.

 "All the resources we need are in the mind."

—Theodore Roosevelt, Jr.

You *can* do what you dream. You may have to change your environment slightly or consider the work in a slightly different capacity, but most dream jobs are attainable. Believe in yourself and you will know that you can do anything you set your heart on. And remember, it is your heart that has the ability to make you happy.

 "Every problem contains the seeds of its own solution."

—Stanley Arnold

Example:

Charlene's dream was to become a professional horse trainer. She wanted to work with champion horses and riders and travel the world with them, but many things seemed to block her path. She had limited horse-training experience and no formal education in the area. Her family thought Charlene was dreaming, and even Charlene herself was not sure if she would like traveling as much as would be required.

Instead of giving up on her dream, however, Charlene decided to try working in a related field. She began volunteering at a local stable and within months was hired to clean stables and do maintenance. Within a year she was working with the horses directly and the following year began assisting with the training.

While these were not championship horses and she was not the head trainer, Charlene was having a great time and was loving her career.

Who knows where Charlene will be in ten years?

Look at "How'd They Get There?" to see how successful people got to where they are today. You may be amazed to discover that most of them started at the bottom and worked their way up.

Consider the variety of occupations related to your dream career. There is sure to be a similar occupation that would fit with your life, skills, education, and ability.

Example:

Dream Job: master chef
Alternative Careers: chef, cook, sous-chef, short-order cook, food server

Dream Job: veterinarian
Alternative Careers: veterinarian's assistant, dog trainer, kennel operator

Dream Job: child psychologist
Alternative Careers: counselor, parenting instructor, daycare operator

You *can* live your dream, maybe slightly differently than you originally thought, but you can do it. Be creative, look at related careers, and commit yourself to following through on your plans.

Never let your dreams die.

 "Alas! the fearful unbelief is unbelief in yourself."

—Thomas Carlyle

Things You Like

There are other things about you besides your dreams that can help you make a career decision. Some basic and important traits that are fundamental to choosing a career are your likes and dislikes. Identifying them will better equip you to look critically at whether or not a career suits you.

An activity you have a passion for may translate into a career. Look into the career opportunities associated with your hobbies. A career counselor or reference librarian can help you get started.

Ask yourself what you like.

✔ Are you a people person or would you rather work with things?

✔ Do you like working with computers? dirt? fabrics? animals? something else?

✔ Would you do shift work?

✔ Would you like to work outside, or do you prefer to work indoors?

✔ What special interests do you have?

Write down things you especially like and things you particularly dislike. These could be anything from "I like worms and dirt" to "I dislike the smell of hospitals." To help you discover what these things are, think about:

✔ hobbies

✔ sports

✔ relationships

✔ school courses

✔ passions

✔ what you do with your leisure time

✔ any other aspects of your life where you have likes and dislikes

Likes

_____ _____ _____
_____ _____ _____
_____ _____ _____
_____ _____ _____
_____ _____ _____

Add to this chart and refer to it as you are considering various occupations.

Dislikes

————————— ————————— —————————
————————— ————————— —————————
————————— ————————— —————————
————————— ————————— —————————
————————— ————————— —————————

By considering your likes and dislikes you may begin to identify jobs that seem interesting or those that are unquestionably "out." This information will also help you to evaluate the suitability of a potential career: does it "fit" with the things you like and dislike?

This information may be as helpful in eliminating potential careers as it is in identifying which ones to pursue.

You may find that, by identifying things you like and dislike, you have significantly increased or reduced the number of careers to consider. This process of adding to your career options and eliminating poor alternatives will eventually result in an informed career decision. You are paving your career path.

"We are not creatures of circumstance; we are creators of circumstance."

—Benjamin Disraeli

Talk, Listen and Learn

Word of mouth is one of the best ways to learn about careers. The more you learn, the better your decision will be. Speak with people about your career dilemma and graciously accept the help and information they provide. This will greatly reduce the amount of work you have to do alone and you may get some ideas you never would have thought of yourself.

 It is a great idea to listen to ideas and suggestions other people have, but remember to evaluate them for yourself. You don't want your career choice to be made by someone else.

Other people, especially family and friends, usually are interested in your career search, particularly if you openly request their input. Use their knowledge and expertise to help make your search for "the career answer" an easier one.

Speak with everyone you can about your career search. This might include:

✔ family

✔ friends

✔ association members

✔ casual acquaintances

✔ friends of friends

✔ professionals

✔ strangers

The more people you talk to, the more people you will have helping you with your search, and the more information you will get.

 Attend company and university open houses. This will help you discover things about jobs, professions, and organizations you may not know about.

Ask people about careers they are familiar with. Use questions such as:

✔ Tell me about your career.

✔ What do you like about your job?

✔ What do you dislike about your work?

✔ If you could do it all over again, would you change anything?

✔ I especially like _____; would these skills/interests be useful in this work?

✔ My interests are _____; do you know of any careers where I could apply these interests?

Any questions encouraging others to "think with you" are good. Chances are, if you ask questions, others will keep their eyes and ears open for you in the future.

Asking questions is more important than asking the perfect question. It is better to begin a discussion with a less-than-perfect question than not to speak with someone at all.

Listen to what people have to say. There is no sense asking them questions if you do not consider what others have to offer. Even if you are not interested in the career being discussed, or if the other person seems to be way out in left field, they may, in passing, say something that piques your interest or leads to a more fruitful discussion.

Be flexible and open when discussing your career with others.

Take a daily planner or notebook everywhere you go to keep track of the information, suggestions and names people give you. You will not forget valuable ideas and will be able to follow up on them later.

Learn from what others are saying.

Example:

After working in a career for two years, Cory was no longer enjoying it. It was still challenging, but it seemed dry and routine.

One day, Cory bumped into a relative who at one time had been in a similar career and the two began discussing Cory's situation. The relative described having had the same problems as Cory was having and gave some suggestions on how to deal with them. Cory was thankful for the suggestions, but had a feeling of déjà vu when they parted.

Several hours later, Cory realized that this relative had described this situation many years before. But at the time Cory hadn't thought he would get bored with his job, so he didn't pay much attention to what his relative had said.

Cory now longed to turn back the hands of time and really listen to their first discussion.

Not everything people tell you will apply to your career, but you never know just what will. Think about what people say they feel about their careers and consider how you would react in similar situations.

Always keep your eyes and ears open for information about careers. People love talking about themselves and you can learn a lot from their experiences and expertise. Comments, suggestions, and ideas from others are as valuable (and usually easier to get) as information from other sources. Use it.

"Perseverance is a great element of success. If you only knock long enough and loud enough at the gate, you are sure to wake up somebody."

—Henry Wadsworth Longfellow

Research and Read

Career programs, educational institutions, private companies, and government agencies have information available to the public on a variety of occupations and careers. It is up to you to take the initiative to find the information and then use it. The reference librarian at your local public library is a great place to get started on your career research.

Literature on careers may provide information about:

✔ typical job descriptions

✔ physical and intellectual demands

✔ work environment

✔ educational requirements

✔ projected growth of the field

✔ related jobs

✔ salary range

✔ companies that hire people in these fields

✔ potential for advancement

✔ other sources of information.

Continue learning as much as you can about careers: the more information you have, the better your choice will be.

"Don't wait for your ship to come;
swim out to it."

—Anonymous

Formal Assistance

An excellent way to obtain help with your career search is by seeking the assistance of a career counselor. A career counselor helps people choose a career by providing information, guidance, and testing. They can help you come up with career alternatives and suggest ways to narrow your options. They will direct you to resources and information that can help with your career search.

Career counselors are familiar with the various aptitude and career evaluation tests. These evaluations are questionnaires that look at your skills, abilities, talents, interests, likes, dislikes, and other aspects of your personality to identify suitable careers for you. These are quick, useful tests that can provide excellent career ideas.

These tests are useful aids but should not be considered "the answer" to all your questions. They have limitations, so don't ever allow a test result to choose your career.

Career counselors are often employed by government-funded employment programs or private career agencies. Find out what services are available in your area and speak with a counselor.

 "Wisely, and slow; they stumble that run fast."

—William Shakespeare

Use the information these tests provide to help identify and narrow your range of options. Be careful not to expect them to tell you what you should be. Remember, it is never a good idea to have someone else choose your career for you, no matter how qualified they seem.

 # Fill a Need

It is always important for you to choose a career you will like, but sometimes an approach different than the one we've just described can be useful. One such approach is to choose a career where you will fill a need.

Often there is a need for products, services, or employees within a company, community, state, or country and this can greatly influence your career. Instead of choosing an occupation and then discovering where you will work, you flip things around. Discover where there is a need and fill it. Using this approach, your career evolves because you have discovered where you are needed.

"The real secret of success is enthusiasm. Yet, more than enthusiasm, I would say excitement. I like to see men get excited. When they get excited they make a success of their lives."

—Walter Chrysler

Example:

Chris was taking a break from the process of choosing a career and went one day to visit his grandfather. He discovered that his grandfather could use help with some of his chores, and after the visit began phoning around to find out who could help him. He was amazed to discover that there were very few agencies providing the services his grandfather required.

Chris began thinking about his own career. He knew he wanted to work with people, but up until now he had no further inclination of what to do. He thought about the needs of his grandfather, and many potential careers came to mind. Chris felt there was a great need for services for elderly people and knew that he had started out on his career journey.

 This does not mean that you should jump into a line of work just because there is a demand for it. Instead, if there is a demand, find work you enjoy that will help to fill a need.

Professionals who advise entrepreneurs suggest they find a product that is in demand, then make and sell it. Provide people with what they want and you will be successful in business. If this is true for business, then it can be true for your career, too. Discover a need, figure out where you fit in, and then begin your career.

Discovering Where You Are Needed

Listen to what is going on around you.

✔ What are the hot issues today? Is there anything you can do to tap into this energy?

✔ Are there products or services not currently available that you could provide?

✔ What needs do people have that your community can't fill?

At times, choosing a career can be as much about "where am I needed?" as about "what will I be?" Keep your eyes and ears open and you may discover where you fit in.

 "I am the master of my fate; I am the captain of my soul."

—William Ernest Henley

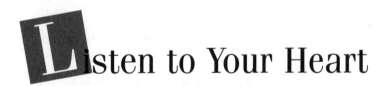 isten to Your Heart

Even after outlining two rational, logical ways of approaching your job search, there may still be some people who have few career ideas. A third approach is to base your decisions less on concrete strategies and more on abstract methods. Your heart, your feelings, and your internal "sense" will help guide you when logic cannot. If you listen to yourself, you may discover your niche.

 "Listen with your heart; you will understand."

—Mother Willow (from *Pocahontas*)

Looking at your career from this perspective means taking a completely different approach. You must be open…open to your thoughts, feelings, ideas, and experiences. You must live, experience, and learn.

Sense…
the things that stimulate you. Become aware of situations and topics that make you "itch" and tug at you to get involved. What topics make you excited and get your adrenaline pumping?

Feel…
what's in your heart. When you feel strongly for or against a subject, think about why. What subjects make you passionate and make you want to voice your opinion?

Discover…
who you are. What kinds of things or people do you like, what gifts do you have, and what skills do you particularly enjoy using? Remember that you have many, many talents, abilities, and gifts, but the key is discovering and using them.

 Always be open to your intuitions and feelings, and when your heart is fighting with your head, listen very closely. Maybe your head is just scared.

There is no way to say where these things will lead you, or how long it will take. You could be led in any of the many directions your heart could take you. You may discover:

✔ what field you want to work in
(working in the health care field so you can help sick people)

✔ what you like doing
(you want to work with the underprivileged)

✔ who you want to work with
(working with children)

✔ where you want to work
(working in the town where you live so you can be close to family and friends)

✔ anything else that feels right in your heart

"Where your treasure is, there will your heart be also."

—Matthew 6:21

Discovering things about yourself is a never ending, amazing, and exciting process, one that is a type of career in itself. Be open to new experiences, new ideas, and to your heart, and discover what is right for you.

Your career is a process, one that evolves and grows as you do.

Allow yourself time to not only experience these things, but to enjoy them as well.

Keeping Opportunity Alive

We discussed in "The Evolution of Career" how you will most likely have different jobs throughout your life and how these jobs will influence future career decisions. You can never know exactly what the future holds, so it is important to watch for new opportunities.

"The secret to success in life is for a man to be ready for his opportunity when it comes."

—Benjamin Disraeli

If you know your skills and the things that interest you, then you will be more responsive when doors open that could lead to a new path in your career. Your career cannot be planned every step of the way, it evolves as you do.

Example:

Alex had been working as a teacher for five years and was very happy. One day he read about an alternative education program for children having trouble in traditional school settings. He read it enthusiastically and thought this was an excellent program.

One year later, Alex's wife accepted a promotion that required them to relocate. When Alex began looking for work he remembered the alternative education program and began looking into what was available in the new city. He found several interesting programs and began working hard to get a job in one of them.

He eventually did.

By being informed and aware of things that interest you, you may discover new aspects to your career. Keep your eyes and ears open, save ideas in the back of your mind, and set your sights on things that will be fun and rewarding.

 Keep a journal where you write down interesting things you have heard about and things you want to try. Refer to it frequently to remind yourself of all the interesting options you have. Follow through on them as opportunities arise.

Opportunities are the doors of change and the way your career can evolve and grow.

Your Choices Are Numerous

By now you should have ideas on careers that are of interest to you. Before you begin to consider which one will be the right choice, remember that a career is a process, one that you will always be working on. The things you do at work, at home, and in your free time will affect the future decisions you make and influence your career as much as the introspective work you are currently doing. Always be open to new ideas.

"Dost thou love life? Then do not squander time, for that's the stuff life is made of."

—Benjamin Franklin

HG

How'd They Get There?
Coreen Mayrs

Coreen Mayrs is the Canadian Casting Director for "The X-Files," one of television's hottest shows, and "Millennium," the new crime-fighting series destined to be equally as popular.

So, how do you get hired to cast not one, but two of the biggest shows on TV? Well, Coreen started with a degree in archaeology! Of her two passions, archaeology and film, Coreen made archaeology her education choice. Within weeks of graduation, however, she volunteered at a commercial production company, was eventually hired, and, starting at the bottom, worked with them in various capacities for two years. Interestingly, the area she knew she was interested in was where she was initially unable to gain work experience: casting. Through persistence and a decision never to take rejection personally, Coreen was finally hired as a casting assistant.

Thriving on challenges and change, Coreen worked her way through the ranks as a casting assistant and extras' casting director. She finally moved into casting for commercials, then movies of the week, and feature films. Indeed, the world of casting has been fast-paced, dynamic, and completely freelance, all aspects Coreen enjoys in her career. There were other jobs along the way, working at a law firm and in a library, but those were times spent learning more about what she didn't want to do in her career than what she did want. Either way, it was a valuable experience. Coreen has always been willing to take risks and admits she has made some bad decisions and some mistakes along the way, but she believes they are necessary in any career—it's how you deal with them that matters.

Still continuing to study, Coreen plans to continue to diversify her career and expand her interests (and she does hope one day to make it onto an archaeological dig!)

If asked to give advice to people choosing their career, Coreen suggests you can do whatever you want in life if you are willing to make sacrifices. The answers are always there for you. Listen to your instincts and persist.

Chapter 4

Uncovering Opportunity

Above all else spend the time and energy you feel you must evaluating your interests and choosing a career you feel fits with your priorities, your goals, and your values. But, before you take the plunge and begin to take progressive leaps toward your dream: did you make certain there is a market for it?

Society today is definitely changing and along with that the career market is also evolving rapidly. As a result, the career you have so carefully planned for since grade school may be on its way to becoming obsolete or may already be extinct.

"Let me tell you the secret that has led me to my goal. My strength lies solely in my tenacity."

—Louis Pasteur

So where does that leave you?

1. You move to the Himalayas to study with a rare group of monks who have yet to make contact with western society,

2. You inform your parents that you plan to live with them indefinitely,

3. You vow to pursue your plans anyway out of respect for the elementary school teacher that inspired your dream,

3. You spend a year in grief and mourning trying to recover from the disappointment.

Okay, maybe not. Instead, you take a deep breath and regroup. This is not the end of the world. You should consider yourself lucky to have done your research ahead of time so you didn't spend four years in college only to find your education obsolete or close to it. This is only a minor setback. Yes, minor.

You know what your interests are and obviously you are fairly certain—if you had already chosen a profession—how your interests translate into a career. So, take those same skills, interests, and abilities and begin to shop around for a new career niche.

Where to Begin

"What I admire in Columbus is not his having discovered a world but his having gone to search for it on the faith of an opinion."

—A. Robert Turgot

With all this talk that the definition of career has taken on a new meaning; that you should expect change in your life, not stability; and that you must expect to be constantly on the lookout for new opportunities for yourself, it would be easy to think that working regularly for a living in a field you enjoy may be close to impossible. It isn't. It's different than it once was, but not impossible.

With every change, no matter how small or how drastic, comes opportunity. You only have to choose to look for it and to be able to see it when it comes your way. It sounds like a challenging task, but you will find that with practice, and with the attitude that you are never "stuck" in one particular job or career, you will soon become a master at uncovering opportunity.

"Luck is being ready for the chance."

—J. Frank Dobie

Identifying Opportunity

How does one recognize a valid career opportunity when it looks like one has come your way?

1. Know your priorities

   Priorities suggest to us what we value in life and what is important enough to us to spend time and energy on. If a career option comes your way, would pursuing it mean you would also be pursuing what is important to you?

 Remember, it is not unusual for your priorities to change with your age. It is likely, therefore, that your career pursuits will change along with your priorities.

2. Know your expectations

   What do you expect your career to provide for you? Money, opportunity to help others, travel options, and so on. Knowing this will make it fairly easy to determine whether or not an option is worth pursuing.

 Be realistic when you are choosing your career. If you expect your career to bring you fame, fortune, health, and guaranteed eternal happiness, you will likely be disappointed.

3. Know yourself

   Can you realistically take on this career move and achieve the kind of success that is important to you? This is a very difficult thing to evaluate sometimes. Be honest with yourself: it will save you considerable energy and stress in the long run.

4. Know your limits

   Are you really willing to put in the time, effort, and commitment that would be necessary to get this opportunity off the ground? It is all too common to find ourselves overwhelmed by a situation we really didn't investigate enough to know we ultimately couldn't handle it.

Each of these points is important in making any kind of decision, but particularly when making one as important as a career choice. Once you begin to understand what is really important to you and what kind of person you are and want to become, you will no doubt find you know right away when an opportunity worth pursuing presents itself.

Although it may seem difficult to you now, make a genuine effort to welcome changes into your life. Trying to "cocoon" and safeguard yourself against changing times and changing circumstances will only make things more difficult for you when you are finally forced to change with the times. Be open to possibilities and enjoy and learn from the new directions your life takes.

"It is a bad plan that admits of no modification."

—Publilius Syrus

Is Opportunity Extinct or Endangered?

Interestingly enough, although large corporations have been downsizing and governments streamlining for at least a decade, many people still expect the economy to return to the way it was. People are hoping for another oil boom or some other driving force that will restore the economic highs we once experienced. Well, as many unemployed and underemployed people can tell you, things are not the way they used to be and it doesn't look like they will be any time soon.

So where does this leave you?

Frankly, it is time to stop hoping for a return to the way things were and start focusing on the way they are. Economies all over the world have changed and it is more difficult to succeed in them. This does not mean, however, there are no opportunities for success. In making your career choice today you must simply do a little more research and a little more forecasting of the future. Opportunity is still out there, it is not an extinct species. You must simply be prepared, above all else, to be flexible.

"To be upset over what you don't have is to waste what you do have."

—Ken S. Keyes, Jr.

Economically Adapting

In our short history review in Chapter One there was some discussion about the post-war economic growth spurt and the baby boomers that came along with it. Once again, that is an interesting place to start.

Why?

Like today, the postwar era signified a drastic change in the economy and people had to adapt. Granted, it was a much more expansive time than now, but it still illustrates some important facts.

What?

The two most important points are that:

- people were faced with a completely new way of doing business and were forced to adapt and,

- it was a time when people with an entrepreneurial spirit were able to forecast into the future to map out their options.

"My interest is in the future because I am going to spend the rest of my life there."

—Charles F. Kettering

What does this have to do with you choosing a career today? Well,

1. Once again people are faced with doing business in a completely new way. True, the opportunities may not be as plentiful as earlier, so in choosing your career direction today, you must understand that you will not likely find a job with one company that will last all your working life. This is an adjustment that everyone entering the world of work will have to come to terms with.

Please remember there are exceptions to every rule.

Additionally,

2. Where at one time it was the entrepreneur at heart who tried to look to the future to determine trends and areas of growth in the economy, now virtually every person hoping to build or expand a career must try to forecast.

The point of all of this is not to make you panic and think you have to run out and buy a crystal ball, or begin to read the world business news every hour on the hour, or try to devise some method to predict the trends of the stock market. The point is to say, once again, the economy is changing. At this time it is not likely that there will be another oil boom or, thankfully, another world war to suddenly feed the economy.

So, the time has come to stop worrying over and longing for what we don't have and start looking at what we do have. There are still areas of growth in the economy. They are perhaps not obvious and, unfortunately, if you know nothing about them they can be a bit intimidating. But, they are there.

 Do a little reading about some past and present businesspeople who became successful by watching trends and trusting their abilities. You may find some helpful inspiration.

Forecasting

Forecasting—for those of us who do not make a profession out of examining trends and waves—quite simply means being aware and being a bit creative.

Okay, technically speaking it means collecting information by examining past and present trends, and using this information to predict what future trends or patterns will be. Sound confusing? Take another look at history.

When the baby boomers were rapidly expanding the population, those with an eye for the future saw this huge number of babies as a key to success. How? By doing a little forecasting—being aware and being creative.

 To help you get an idea of how the boomers affected the economy, try this: Picture a normal economy as a regular garden hose with lumps and bumps and the occasional kink in it. Now, think of the huge population of baby boomers traveling through our economy as a football going through that garden hose. That should give you some idea of the numbers and, more importantly, the effect such numbers of people would have (and are still having) on the economy.

So, businesspeople who have pictured the boomer population coming through the hose, and who have been able to predict what kind of products and services the "football" will need and want, have been very successful indeed.

Example:

1. The time: late 1950s. You are in the restaurant business and realize that society and peoples' needs are changing and you are being left behind. The boomers are now children and young teens. Their parents are people with some expendable income and a busy schedule with their new families. Being an entrepreneur, you do a little brainstorming, talk to some people you know who have some money to invest in your project, and decide to open a new type of restaurant.

   You tell your investors you want to cater to the slightly faster-paced, slightly busier lifestyle of the boomer family. You want to appeal to the kids in those families, whose parents are trying to feed and please them. What do you do? You create a fast-food hamburger joint, with some fuzzy, fun mascots to entertain the kids. You fill a need with your restaurant.

   The result: McDonald's restaurants are born.

Example:

2. The time: late 1970s. The boomers now have kids of their own and they also have some money to spend on them. You are a creative business student and you start to do some forecasting of your own.

   As every generation does, the boomers want their kids to have more things and more advantages than they did, and that means everything from getting a good education to having all the latest toys. You take on the challenge and build a computer in the garage in your back yard. It's fun, it's easy to use, and parents can buy it for their kids for fun or for education. You start to sell a few.

   The result: Apple computers are born.

 Obviously there was a lot of time and hard work invested in both of these companies. The point is that there was a need to be filled and there were people who took the risk to succeed at filling it.

Another history lesson complete! So, are you getting the idea? Both of these examples—and there are hundreds more, from baby food to running shoes—are of people and companies who were not necessarily successful when they began, but who looked around them, took some risks, and were ultimately incredibly successful.

That, in essence, is what forecasting is all about:

1. Know your skills and what you have to offer

2. Observe trends in society

3. Evaluate the needs of specific groups in society

4. Decide if and for how long that need can be filled

5. Create the necessary service or product

6. Start working and fill that need

When doing your forecasting homework, start with your interests. Something that is an interest or hobby for you may be of interest to a much larger market. Dream big!

Now more than ever, with many companies and entire industries downsizing into virtual nonexistence, you need to take a look at which industries are expanding or have the potential to expand. When you decide what those are, you can begin to research where you and your skills can fit in and succeed.

Is There Growth Out There?

With all this talk of downsizing and change, this is a valid question.

The answer is, yes.

Remember, the growth industries in the '90s are generally not the huge corporations, but rather the small businesses set up to fill specific needs in specific markets. This is where the economy is growing. As people like yourself become frustrated with the uncertainty of corporate life, more individuals and groups are pooling their ideas and resources and setting up shop for themselves.

If you find yourself depressed over job cutbacks and layoffs, stop reading the paper so much. Get out and talk to people and you may find that those people who are victims of layoffs are also those who are starting the local Internet cafe or trendy health club for seniors.

One unfortunate drawback for people wanting to choose a career in a growth industry is that the smaller the business the harder it is to research. This simply means you may have to get out and meet the people directly in those businesses you think may interest you, rather than reading about them at the library or on the Internet. Put on your shoes and get out there and see who is working, who is successful, what they are doing, and how they got there. Be creative, innovative, and persistent!

 As with networking of any sort, start with your interests. Look in the telephone directory, talk to people you know, and read community news bulletins and flyers to find out what's new and who's doing it.

Other Considerations

It is one thing to tell you that you need to evaluate trends, fill needs, and make yourself as diverse as possible in today's changing career market. But there are a few other things you need to consider personally.

What?

Location:

Where you want to live may influence your career choice considerably. Many careers are widely available, but some are definitely more limited in location. If you decide retail sales is for you, you can most likely do this almost anywhere. Becoming a grain buyer, however, will require you to move to the part of the country where the grain is grown.

If you haven't yet decided on your career path, think about where you want to live. Are you willing to move to another town, city, state, or region, or is it important for you to live in a specific location? Consider all of these things: they will influence your career choices.

Decide now if there are any restrictions on where you want to live. There is no sense in training for a specific career if you aren't willing to move to where that career is in demand.

Shift work:

Police officers, firefighters, factory workers, journalists, nurses, and many others are required to work shifts during their careers. This is most definitely a consideration when choosing your career.

Any career that requires you to work shifts may also require you to make some considerable adjustments in your lifestyle. You need to decide what is important to you when faced with the possibility of working shifts, and how it will affect your health, family, social life, and other activities. It is one thing to be certain you would enjoy the career itself. It is quite another to find yourself a year into your new job not being able to cope with how your work schedule is affecting your life.

"It is the first of all problems for a man to find out what kind of work he is to do in this universe."

—Thomas Carlyle

Rate of Pay:

Although we have stressed thus far in the book that people must not let their quest for financial gain rule their lives, you also must be realistic. Money is necessary in life and obviously an important factor in any career.

Take the time when you are choosing a career to do a salary survey to determine how much money people in the industry make. Then, take the time to really look at how much money you feel you need to maintain the style of life you desire. If there is too large a difference between the numbers, you may have to consider choosing another career and turn your first choice into a hobby or part-time job.

Other factors such as hours of work, vacation time, work environment, and flexibility will affect your career choice. Take the time to think about how you feel about all of these things.

The Time Line

Right from the time we enter school, it seems people ask us what we want to be when we grow up. At the time, it doesn't seem like such a tough question. We know what we like, we know who we admire, and that's what we want to do.

Well, as we approach the dying days of high school and have to start thinking about work or about college, suddenly that question doesn't seem so straightforward and we don't feel very grown-up! Needless to say, it can be a very stressful time for those who are not destined to be concert pianists or star forwards for the varsity basketball team.

 "In every fear there is a desire."
—Freud

Don't panic.

Although sometimes it seems like it, there is no rule written that says we have to come out of high school knowing exactly what we want to study in college and exactly what career that will lead us into. Yes, you will be pressured by your parents and maybe by your teachers and your friends, but don't be too hard on yourself. There are a lot of things to consider and there is still some time to consider them.

If you aren't sure coming out of high school exactly what direction you want to go in, try some things, get some experience. Get a job in a restaurant, work part time if you can for Uncle Gerome or Aunt Margaret, pick up some shifts as a laborer on a construction site, see if you can work in the mail room at a big corporation. No, you're right, these aren't glamorous, high-paying jobs, but they are jobs that will help you determine what you do and don't want to do in your career. They will earn you a little cash and teach you a whole lot about what direction you want to take.

If this isn't your first career choice you probably have a better idea of what you like and what you don't. Still, it wouldn't hurt to take some classes or one-day seminars, do some investigation.

If you still find yourself at a loss as to what you want to do with your life, there are some other techniques you can try.

First:

Stop thinking of it as "what you want to do with the rest of your life." That in itself is enough to paralyze anyone with fear. There is nothing written anywhere that says you only get one chance to make this decision and you can never again change your mind.

 Take the time to consider if it is your ego that is getting in your way. Are you feeling like you should be an instant success at whatever you do? Success is a process.

Now:

Give yourself a break. Sometimes just forgetting about the problem for a time is enough to help you with your decision. Remember, "a time" doesn't mean forever. You will have to decide eventually.

 Taking a break assumes you have put some time and energy already into researching your options.

Next:

Accept that whatever decision you make will not be absolutely perfect forever. There will be things about whichever career you choose you like or dislike. Accept this and quit trying to choose the "ultimate" career.

Then:

Dream a little more. Let your imagination run wild and come up with any and every bizarre, exciting, unusual, and crazy career possibility you have ever thought of. This will help you relax and it will also help you remember what your interests are and what your true feelings about career are.

Finally:

Do whatever it is you do when you are feeling a little down, when your self-confidence maybe needs a boost. Decision making of any kind takes self-confidence. So, if you are having some trouble with your decision, try a confidence booster, it may be just what you need.

 If you try all these things and still feel at a loss, reevaluate your priorities. Write them down and really take a look at what type of career would fit with them.

n Conclusion

Choosing a career, despite the title of this book, is not a completely painless procedure. It will take time and energy, some soul-searching and honest self-evaluation, and a lot of work to decide in which direction you want to lead your life.

True, the world is a changing place and you will have to change along with it if you want to be successful. You know that careers are different creatures than they once were and perhaps not quite so easy to come by. This *does not* mean it is impossible to find a productive, satisfying, sufficiently challenging, and rewarding career that will fit in with your dreams, goals and priorities.

Above all else, remember that there are no guarantees. You have to make your own success and at times you will find that overwhelming. Don't despair, you will work through the decisions and the changes that you have to make and you will make progress because of that.

There will be times when you wish someone would just tell you what you should do and you could just go out and do it. What would be the adventure in that?

What is there left to say?

"Whatever you can do or dream you can, begin it. Boldness has genius, power and magic in it. Begin it now."

Johann Wolfgang von Goethe

That Was Then...

- Choosing a career, if you were a man, often meant doing what your father did.

- If you were a woman, generally your career choices were seriously limited. Women's careers were often as teachers, nurses, home-makers, and mothers.

- An education was a luxury.

- Unless that job unexpectedly ended, you had one job (you probably never called it a career) for all your working life.

- You were more likely to have a physically demanding job, or one working with people rather than working with technology.

- Although you may have had to travel to find work, it was likely you didn't leave your region or state—very rarely did you have to leave the country.

- Often you didn't actually make a conscious career choice. Instead, you found a job, or happened into one, liked it, and stayed with it.

- You spoke with people about "how you made a living," not about your career.

 Whether we mean for it to happen or not, our parents are often very influential in our career decision-making process. Keep in mind that the career market for you today may be quite different from when they were starting out.

This Is Now...

- Education is essential.

- Your options are too numerous to count whether you are a man or a woman.

- You could just as easily move to a new country as a new city to find a career you enjoy.

- Technology is one of the fastest growing industries, which means if you are looking for a growth career, it is likely that you will be looking to technology.

- You will almost definitely change jobs at least five times in your working life; you may change careers that many times as well.

- You may juggle more than one type of career at any one time in your employment history.

- Your career history reveals a variety of jobs and positions often reflecting the economic times and your outlook.

"There's a deep tendency in human nature to become precisely what we imagine or picture ourselves to be."

—Norman Vincent Peale

Conclusion

Ideas generated, career paths thought through, research complete…
you're on the next leg of your career journey. Enjoy whatever occupation you choose and remember that each job has its place in your career path. Your career, like life, is a journey to be enjoyed and relished.

"We must dare, and dare again,
and go on daring."

—George Jacques Danton

VGM CAREER BOOKS

BUSINESS PORTRAITS
Apple
Boeing
Coca-Cola
Ford
Kellogg's
McDonald's

CAREER DIRECTORIES
Careers Encyclopedia
Dictionary of Occupational Titles
Occupational Outlook Handbook

CAREERS FOR
Animal Lovers; Bookworms; Car Buffs;
Caring People; Computer Buffs; Crafty
People; Culture Lovers; Environmental
Types; Fashion Plates; Film Buffs; Foreign
Language Aficionados; Good Samaritans;
Gourmets; Health Nuts; History Buffs;
Kids at Heart; Music Lovers; Mystery
Buffs; Nature Lovers; Night Owls;
Number Crunchers; Plant Lovers; Self-
Starters; Shutterbugs; Sports Nuts; the
Stagestruck; Travel Buffs; Writers

CAREERS IN
Accounting; Advertising; Business; Child
Care; Communications; Computers;
Education; Engineering; the
Environment; Finance; Government;
Health Care; High Tech; Horticulture &
Botany; International Business;
Journalism; Law; Marketing; Medicine;
Science; Social & Rehabilitation Services;
Travel, Tourism, & Hospitality

CAREER PLANNING
Beating Job Burnout
Beginning Entrepreneur
Big Book of Jobs
Career Planning & Development for
College Students & Recent Graduates
Career Change
Career Success for People with Physical
Disabilities
Careers Checklists
College and Career Success for Students
with Learning Disabilities
Complete Guide to Career Etiquette
Cover Letters They Don't Forget
Dr. Job's Complete Career Guide
Executive Job Search Strategies
Guide to Basic Cover Letter Writing
Guide to Basic Resume Writing
Guide to Internet Job Searching
Guide to Temporary Employment
Job Interviewing for College Students
Joyce Lain Kennedy's Career Book
Out of Uniform
Parent's Crash Course in Career Planning

Slam Dunk Cover Letters
Slam Dunk Resumes
Up Your Grades: Proven Strategies for
Academic Success

CAREER PORTRAITS
Animals; Cars; Computers; Electronics;
Fashion; Firefighting; Food; Music;
Nature; Nursing; Science; Sports;
Teaching; Travel; Writing

GREAT JOBS FOR
Art Majors
Business Majors
Communications Majors
Engineering Majors
English Majors
Foreign Language Majors
History Majors
Liberal Arts Majors
Psychology Majors
Sociology Majors

HOW TO
Apply to American Colleges and
Universities
Approach an Advertising Agency and Walk
Away with the Job You Want
Be a Super Sitter
Bounce Back Quickly After
Losing Your Job
Change Your Career
Choose the Right Career
Cómo escribir un currículum vitae en
inglés que tenga éxito
Find Your New Career Upon Retirement
Get & Keep Your First Job
Get Hired Today
Get into the Right Business School
Get into the Right Law School
Get into the Right Medical School
Get People to Do Things Your Way
Have a Winning Job Interview
Hit the Ground Running in Your New
Job
Hold It All Together When You've Lost
Your Job
Improve Your Study Skills
Jumpstart a Stalled Career
Land a Better Job
Launch Your Career in TV News
Make the Right Career Moves
Market Your College Degree
Move from College into a
Secure Job
Negotiate the Raise You Deserve
Prepare Your Curriculum Vitae
Prepare for College
Run Your Own Home Business

Succeed in Advertising When all You
Have Is Talent
Succeed in College
Succeed in High School
Take Charge of Your Child's Early
Education
Write a Winning Resume
Write Successful Cover Letters
Write Term Papers & Reports
Write Your College Application Essay

MADE EASY
Choosing a Career
College Applications
Cover Letters
Getting a Raise
Job Hunting
Job Interviews
Resumes

ON THE JOB: REAL PEOPLE WORKING IN...
Communications
Health Care
Sales & Marketing
Service Businesses

OPPORTUNITIES IN
This extensive series provides detailed
information on more than 150 individual career fields.

RESUMES FOR
Advertising Careers
Architecture and Related Careers
Banking and Financial Careers
Business Management Careers
College Students &
Recent Graduates
Communications Careers
Computer Careers
Education Careers
Engineering Careers
Environmental Careers
Ex-Military Personnel
50+ Job Hunters
First-Time Job Hunters
Government Careers
Health and Medical Careers
High School Graduates
High Tech Careers
Law Careers
Midcareer Job Changes
Nursing Careers
Performing Arts Careers
Re-Entering the Job Market
Sales and Marketing Careers
Science Careers
Scientific and Technical Careers
Social Service Careers

VGM Career Horizons
a division of *NTC/Contemporary Publishing*
4255 West Touhy Avenue
Lincolnwood, Illinois 60646–19753